# Glossary of Search Fund Terms

## How to speak the language of Entrepreneurship through Acquisition

Newton M. Campos, Ph.D.
Paulo R. M. Abreu
Carlos Gila
Jhonathan Doria

**1st Edition, 3rd Revision**
Copyright © 2024
Newton M. Campos, Paulo R. M. Abreu,
Carlos Gila, Jhonathan Doria.
Publisher: Amazon's KDP Print self-publishing platform. USA.
Original Publishing Date: April 17th, 2022.
Publishing Date, 3rd Revision: Jan 10th, 2024.
ISBN: 9798806938085

# Preface

It was around May 2014, when after scheduling a call with a former alumnus of mine, we had the chance to update each other about our lives: I had recently returned to Brazil, and he had gone to finish his MBA at Yale University in the United States. Right at the beginning of the call, he tells me: "I'm working for a Search Fund and we're buying a company in the Dominican Republic."

I took advantage of the call to learn as much as I could about Search Funds. I was immediately impressed by the model. As the son of a serial entrepreneur and myself an accountant and small business owner at different points of my life, I identified with the model almost immediately. The Search Fund, born in the academic world that I had embraced with affection since my PhD years, combined the thirst for entrepreneurship that some people have with the thirst for investment that other people develop by managing, inheriting, or accumulating resources in different ways.

All of this in a more discreet and tangible world, far from the spotlight of "miraculous" Startups and the "seductive" Private Equity funds. At the end, the model is simple to understand: One or two professionals with a strong desire to lead in an entrepreneurial way seek and locate a healthy medium-sized company, acquire it with the support of investors and build up a new history for this company, taking advantage of the full potential of its collaborators, products, brands, customers, and suppliers to make it bigger and more relevant to society.

These young people (known as Searchers) become partners in the company from day one, in the role of CEOs, learning high-level leadership on the job, with the support of some of the experienced investors who put their money to back them up. In the sale of the acquired company, several years after the acquisition, carried out almost always for an amount well above the purchase price, everyone wins and sets out to new challenges. The country gains a bigger and more promising business with more jobs, more qualified people, more taxes paid and more satisfied customers.

Every industry adopts a specific vocabulary that facilitates and speeds up information exchange and transactions. Search Funds are no different; although the vocabulary comes overwhelmingly from the Private Equity industry, there are some twists. Proudly prepared by researchers from Europe and Latin America, the Glossary of Search Fund Terms was designed to support this emerging industry around the world, where not only new Searchers and Investors seek to innovate through the companies they acquire, but also lawyers, accountants, brokers, and other stakeholders try to learn the language of Entrepreneurship through Acquisition.

Newton M. Campos, Ph.D.

# Acknowledgments

This glossary would not be possible without the collaboration and dedication of many individuals and organizations. Without financial sponsorships of any kind, we, the four main authors Dr. Newton M. Campos (affiliated to FGV EAESP and IE University as Adjunct Professor), Paulo R. M. Abreu (FGV EAESP and IE University alumnus), Carlos Gila (affiliated to Columbia University and IE University as Adjunct Professor) and Jhonathan Doria (Insper alumnus), along with Vani Nadarajah (Fletcher alumnus) and Felipe A. Camara (FGV EAESP alumnus) as research assistants, spent more than 300 hours compiling more than 250 financial terms mostly used by the Private Equity industry and adapting them to the reality of Search Funds around the world. For this revised edition, more terms were added to the more than 200 original ones that were also revised and updated, as we received the support of the prestigious Brazilian law firm FM/Derraik, in special from Cristiana Rebelo Wiener and André G. Fabri.

Equivalent to more than a month of full-time equivalent work, executed by highly trained academics and professionals, our dream to contribute to this emerging field in Entrepreneurship is now a reality. We hope that

Entrepreneurs as well as investors, lawyers, accountants, Family Offices, M&A professionals, brokers, family business owners and all professionals increasingly impacted by the growth of Search Funds worldwide value our effort and count on us to push responsible entrepreneurial leadership up to a new level.

We would like to acknowledge the official support of FGV, its Research Committee and Prof. Dr. Edgard Barki, head of FGVcenn Center for Entrepreneurship and New Busines at FGV EAESP who provided a safe and known rigorous research environment that allowed our Research Team to develop this relevant piece of knowledge for Entrepreneurship though Acquisition enthusiasts. Opinions expressed in this work are the responsibility of the authors and do not necessarily reflect the opinions of FGV EAESP or its supporters.

The Research Team

# Introduction

Writing a glossary is not an easy task: Which terms should we include or exclude? How detailed should each entry be? Should we include examples? What about synonyms and cross references? For these reasons, we made some important decisions to allow for a better reading experience.

The entries were decided and described for people with a basic to intermediary business vocabulary. Therefore, the glossary will mainly help professionals that are already doing business, but with limited knowledge of the Private Equity & Venture Capital traditional vocabulary. We aimed to be succinct so that readers can look for more information elsewhere, once an entry triggers their interest.

Pitchbook, Investopedia and Divestopedia were the main sources for the entries but most of them were adapted by the research team to the reality of Search Funds in the first quarter of the 21st century (CE). Additionally, sources such as the Stanford Search Fund studies, as well as publications as diverse as Preqin or The Economist were used sometimes.

We also decided to keep the references at the end of the document, to facilitate the reading of the whole text in an hour or two. Most of the references are clickable, to facilitate an early, independent investigation of specific terms.

We hope that you enjoy reading this glossary with the same pleasure that we all had while researching the terms, adapting them, and finally editing them for good readability and further research. We believe that the more accessible the Entrepreneurial Process is by people from around the world, the more Entrepreneurship through Acquisition will become a way to innovate and make the world a better place.

If this glossary helps responsible entrepreneurs to meet responsible investors, then we will know that our work was not in vain.

The Research Team

Page intentionally left blank.

# A

**Accelerator** (*see also* **Incubator**): A program, organization or individual Searchers can apply to receive support. Accelerators provide funds, mentorship and/or acquisition pipeline, among other kinds of support to help Searchers acquire and run the acquired company, usually in exchange for 40-60% of the Searcher's equity. *Reference [1] adapted by authors.*

**Acquisition Capital:** Typical Search Fund's second round of fundraising after the Searching phase in order to acquire a company. Self-funded Search Fund will only raise Acquisition Capital. In Search Funds the acquisition price usually ranges from US$5m to US$25, or below the lowest end of the Private Equity check size in a particular country. Depending on each deal and country the Acquisition Capital will represent something in between 40-60% of the acquisition price. *Reference [2] adapted by authors.*

**Add-on and Bolt-on:** When a Private Equity backed firm acquires a company to add onto an existing portfolio company. In add-on deals, the existing portfolio company is called the platform and the Private Equity firm is called the sponsor. Bolt-on is a term used more often in Europe. Despite

Search Fund targets to acquire only one business, the acquired company often benefit from Add-ons and M&A to grow. *Reference [1] adapted by authors.*

**Agency Costs or Agency Risk:** Type of internal company expense, which comes from the actions of a company's management (CEO and other key managers) acting on its own interest or on behalf of one or more specific shareholders in situations where there is a difference of interest between management and shareholders. Agency Costs typically arise in the wake of core inefficiencies, dissatisfaction, and disruptions such as conflicts of interest between management and shareholders and may lead to substantial additional costs or the loss of value. In Search Funds, Agency Costs might emerge, for example, when the management, in its own behalf, or along with specific investors or board members, force lower revenues to lower the valuation of the company before exit, in the intention of buying it at a better price. This reduction in value is an Agency Cost. *Reference [93] adapted by authors.*

**Agnostic investment:** Investment in any company or geographic region that expects to go well in a particular country. In this case, the investor doesn't specialize in a specific industry or geographic region and applies its knowledge, products, processes, technologies, and resources in different industries instead of only few ones. In some cases, however, while industry agnostic firms may work in several different industries, they still have a geographic or a specific Check Size focus. *Reference authors.*

**Alternative investment:** An asset that is not a conventional investment type (stocks, bonds, gold, etc.). Alternative investments include Search Funds, Venture Capital, Private Equity, Hedge Funds, Arts collections, legal assets, and Real Estate. *References [1, 3] adapted by authors.*

**Amortization:** Payment of debt installments or a series of payments received due on invested capital. *Reference [4] adapted by authors.*

**Angel investor:** A high-net-worth individual (HNWI) who makes direct investments into early-stage businesses or Search Capital. *Reference [1].*

**Anti-embarrassment clause:** Also known as on-sale, is a clause that enables the seller to recalculate the purchase price of a share and subject it to an increase in the event that the buyer sells the same shares at a higher price. This clause is valid only for a certain period of time following the completion of a particular transaction. This clause is mostly used in share purchase agreements. Rarely are anti-embarrassment clauses negotiated in the sale of a mid-market business because it is unlikely that a company could be subsequently sold to another buyer in a relatively short period of time. *Reference [5].*

**Anti-trust filing:** A formal notification of an acquisition to competition regulators. *Reference [1].*

**Asset allocation:** The mix of investments in a portfolio. To balance risk and reward, asset allocation is determined by investment goals, risk tolerance and time. *Reference [1].*

**Asset class:** Group of financial instruments with similar characteristics usually organized by categories. Search Funds constitute one specific kind of asset class within the Private Equity spectrum. *Reference [6] adapted by authors.*

**Asset deal:** When the assets of a company are acquired instead of shares. *Reference [1].*

**Asset-based lending:** Any form of lending to a business that is collateralized or secured by a balance sheet asset. Pledged assets may include inventory, equipment or accounts receivable that will be redeemed in the event of default by the debtor. *Reference [1].*

# B

**Baskets:** In the context of Private Equity and Venture Capital, the term basket typically refers to a "management fee" basket or "transaction expenses" basket. These baskets are used to account for certain fees and expenses associated with managing the investment fund or executing transactions. The "management fee" basket refers to a provision in a Private Equity or Venture Capital fund's limited partnership agreement. The Management fee basket allows the general partner (GP) to counterbalance some of the management fees charged to the fund against future profits or distributions to investors (limited partners or LPs). A "transaction expenses" basket is used to account for certain expenses related to the deals. These expenses might include legal fees, due diligence costs, and other expenses incurred during the process of acquiring or investing in a portfolio company. The basket sets a threshold for these expenses, and it's typically assumed by the acquiring company (portfolio company) or the investment fund. Once the expenses exceed the basket amount, they may become the responsibility of the seller or subject to negotiation between the parties. In Search Funds, the Search Capital should cover all costs associated with the search, including two to three due diligences while the

Acquisition Capital follow the terms of the Purchasing Agreement. If the search results in no acquisition after 24 to 30 months, a new Search Capital round might be raised against the searcher future carried interest. *Reference authors.*

**Benchmark:** When a fund compares its returns to the performance of similar funds. *Reference [1].*

**Binding Offer and Non-Binding Offer:** A Binding Offer refers to an offer made by a bidder to acquire a target company (or seller) after the due diligence phase of a sale process is complete. This offer constitutes a formal contract between the bidder and seller should the seller accept the bidder's terms and the acquisition has to be honored if due diligence confirms promised data about the company. A Non-Binding Offer does not require the deal to be concluded even if the due diligence confirms the promised data. *Reference [7] adapted by authors.*

**Board of directors:** A group of individuals selected to represent stockholders with regard to company policies or significant company decisions. In Search Funds, a board of 3 members is usually constituted, with board members representing all the investors in the company's decisions. In Search Funds, generally board members receive an annual remuneration of US$10 to US$18 thousand dollars paid by the acquired company. *Reference [1] adapted by authors.*

**Book runner:** The main entity responsible for the issuance of new equity, debt, and other securities. *Reference [1].*

**Break-up fee:** A break-up fee is paid in an acquisition by the party that decides not to pursue the deal (e.g., a Binding Offer). The break-up fee can be paid to either the buyer or the seller. A seller may ask for a break-up fee if not completing the deal would have a negative consequence on the seller, if the sales process is disruptive to the operation of the business, or when the seller has been approached with an unsolicited offer. A break-up fee offered in the letter of intent (LOI) will show the buyer's commitment to completing the acquisition. *References [8, 9] adapted by authors.*

**Bridge loan:** A temporary, limited amount of financing that serves as a 'bridge' until a long-term debt or equity investment can be secured. It is used by some Search Fund investors to allow deals to occur when their capital calls delay in time. *Reference [1] adapted by authors.*

**Broker:** A group of financial advisors or M&A boutiques that intermediates financial transactions and usually they are paid by commissions on the transaction value. *Reference [10] adapted by authors.*

**Brownfield:** An investment in an existing asset, land or structure that typically requires repairs, upgrades, and expansion. *Reference [1].*

**Burn rate:** How long it takes a company to spend the capital it received from investors. *Reference [1].*

**Business development company:** A company created to invest in both the debt and equity of small and medium-sized enterprises (SMEs). Investments can be made in both public and private entities. While similar to VC funds, many BDCs are publicly traded, which allows smaller, non-accredited investors to back SMEs. *Reference [1] adapted by authors.*

**Buy-and-build:** A buy and build strategy is typically deployed by Private Equity to generate value and increase their returns. It entails buying a platform company with established management and systems and leveraging off this company to acquire subsequent tuck-in acquisitions. *Reference [11].*

**Buyout or Leveraged buyout:** A Private Equity transaction in which a firm acquires all - or a significant amount of - equity in a company. A leveraged buyout is when firms use a mix of cash and debt to acquire equity, which in Search Funds is very common in developed economies but rarer in developing economies. *Reference [1].*

# C

**CAGR (Compound Annual Growth Rate):** Is the rate of return (RoR) that would be required for an investment to grow from its beginning balance to its ending balance, assuming the profits were reinvested at the end of each period of the investment's life span. *Reference [12].*

**CAIA (Certified Alternative Investments A):** Certified Alternative Investments A. Certification for professionals in Alternative Investments. *Reference [13].*

**Call Option and Call Option Notice:** A Call Option is a right (but not an obligation) for its owner to purchase a specified number of shares or securities at a specified price for a fixed or indefinite period. The holder of the Call Option right exercises his or her rights by means of a Call Option Notice generally to the issuer of the shares or securities. *Reference authors.*

**CapEx (Capital Expenditures):** Capital expenditures (CapEx) are funds used by a company to acquire, upgrade, and maintain physical assets such as property, plants, buildings, technology, or equipment. CapEx is often used to undertake new projects or investments by a company. In Search Funds,

CapEx intensive companies are generally avoided as they require extra investments other than the Acquisition Capital to keep growing. *Reference [14] adapted by authors.*

**Capital call:** When a General Partner (managers of a fund) is ready to make an investment, it will ask its Limited Partners (owners of the money) for the capital they have already committed to the fund. *Reference [1] adapted by authors.*

**Capital overhang** (*see* **Dry powder**).

**Cap table:** Current list a company's participation status by shareholder. In Search Funds the Cap table is a key aspect of the model as both Searcher(s) and Investors try to organize a balanced Cap table for both financing stages. For Search Capital, Searchers need a combination of Investors that can: help them in analyzing the possible deals as they mature; provide guidance in the different stages of search; open up room for equity gaps in the acquisition so that industry focused Investors can join the Cap table; have enough capital to cover eventual equity gaps or bring financing options for a leveraged acquisition. For Acquisition Capital, Searchers need a combination of Investors that can: help them running the company from a strategic, industry, technological or sustainable point of view; provide guidance in the different stages of value creation; provide extra capital for growth when needed; help them in providing good exit strategies. *Reference authors.*

**Carried interest:** A General Partner's share of the capital gains from a fund, usually 20%. *Reference [1].*

**Carve-out (***see also* **Spin-off):** When a company sells all or part of its business to new owners. A Carve-out allows a company to capitalize on a business segment that may not be part of its core operations. Unlike a Spin-off, the parent company generally receives a cash inflow through a Carve-out. *Reference [1] adapted by authors.*

**Ceteris paribus:** Latin expression meaning "all other things being equal" or "other things held constant". Used in Science, Economics and Law to refer to a causal, often empirical, or logical relationship between two physical, economic, or legal states or variables.

**Change of control clauses:** Clauses that can invalidate or dissolve a contract in the event that a change in control of the company takes place. *Reference [1].*

**Chairman:** Member of a corporation's board of directors or an advisory committee who presided over its meetings and in some cases may have a casting vote when there is a tie within the board or the committee. *Reference authors.*

**Chapter 11:** The section of the US Bankruptcy Code that outlines the process for asset reorganization. *Reference [1].*

**Chapter 7:** The section of the US Bankruptcy Code that outlines the process for asset liquidation. *Reference [1].*

**Check Size:** Refers to the amount of money an investor is willing to invest in a single deal or company. In Search Funds, it refers to the amount invested in acquiring the company after the search phase is complete. This amount varies in between $200 thousand $2 million, based on the size and profitability of the target company and the equity aimed by the investor. The check size is generally much smaller than typical Private Equity investments, because multiple investors tend to enter in a Search Fund deal. *Reference authors.*

**CIM (Confidential Information Memorandum) or IM (Information Memorandum):** Document used in M&A (Mergers and Acquisitions) to convey important information about a business that's for sale including its operations, financial statements, management team, and other data to a prospective buyer. *Reference [15].*

**Closed fund:** A fund that has finished taking strong commitments from Limited Partners and is ready to make investments. *Reference [1] adapted by authors.*

**Closing account:** An account that helps determine the net debt and working capital that will be used to establish the final price of an M&A deal according to the agreed price formula. *Reference [1].*

**Closing agreement:** A document that establishes the final settlement between all parties involved in an M&A deal and results in the transfer of ownership from, and payment to, the target company. *Reference [1].*

**Club Deal:** Also known as a consortium or syndicated investment, is when two or more Private Equity firms, Family Offices or other investors jointly purchase a business. Club Deals allow Private Equity firms to compete for acquisition targets that were once only available to larger strategic acquirers, while reducing risk exposure to any one member at the same time. A Club Deal is also used to define a type of syndicated loan provided by a group of lenders on an M&A transaction. While in Search Funds the search and acquisition processes are led by a Searcher under standardized practices, in Club Deals the process is led by investors under a variety of circumstances. *References [16, 17] adapted by authors.*

**Coachable Searcher:** Refers to a Searcher capable of being easily taught and trained to do something better or something different. In the Search Fund industry, a Coachable Searcher is an individual with transferable skills sets, capable of learning or developing new skills at a fast pace in a particular industry or field. In the Search Fund model, you have on one side, the Searcher who is young, motivated, gifted, but inexperienced as a CEO, and the investors, who act as coaches or mentors and advise the Searcher during the Search Fund trajectory. *Reference authors.*

**Co-investment:** A fundamental aspect of Search Funds. Searchers locate and choose a group of 10 to 20 investors to finance the search and acquisition of a business. *Reference authors.*

**Completion accounts** (*see also* **Locked Box**): In a transaction, a completion mechanism is used to determine the final acquisition price that the buyer must pay in order to acquire the shares of the target company. There is more than one way of doing this and the outcome can be different depending on the mechanism used. There are two widely accepted mechanisms for adjusting the consideration: "Completion Accounts" and "Locked Box". In a Completion Accounts scenario, the "initial" acquisition price is defined in the signed Share Purchase Agreement (or SPA). However, the "final" acquisition price is only determined based on the actual balance sheet of the target entity prepared as at the date of completion of the transaction. As a minimum, the Completion Accounts show the net assets of the acquired business as at the date of completion. Typically, they will comprise a closing balance sheet, and will usually include a profit and loss account showing the results for the period from the latest set of historical financial accounts up to the completion date. A major advantage of Completion Accounts approach is that it provides the possibility of the acquisition price being adjusted on a Euro-for-Euro basis. This simultaneously entails the mechanism's major disadvantage since major adjustments to the initial acquisition price often led to time-consuming discussions between the buyer and the seller and generate uncertainty as to whether the takeover will succeed after all. *Reference [18].*

**Condition precedent:** A condition for closing a negotiated agreement such as securing approval from regulators. *Reference [1].*

**Convertible debt:** Debt that can be converted to equity when certain conditions are met, like a specific valuation or date. *Reference [1].*

**Corporate acquisition:** When a corporation purchases another company for strategic purposes. *Reference [1].*

**Corporate Venture Capital:** When a corporation has a Venture Capital team that invests in early-stage companies aligned with the corporation's goals. *Reference [1].*

**Crowdfunded Search:** Less typical structure for Search Funds with a few precedents in USA where the Searcher partially raises the Search capital through general investors (usually in online platforms) looking for exposure to the asset class. *Reference [19].*

**Crowdfunding:** The process of raising small amounts of capital from many people to fund a venture. *Reference [1].*

# D

**Data room or Virtual Data Room:** A secure, digital location where potential investors can review confidential information on a target company, including financial statements, compensation agreements, intellectual property, and client contracts. The Data Room is an integral part of the due diligence process, which takes place after a non-disclosure agreement has been signed. It is also known as "Due Diligence Data Room". *References [1, 20].*

**De Minimis:** A legal term meaning too small to be meaningful or taken into consideration. As a matter of policy, the law does not encourage parties to bring legal actions for technical breaches of rules or agreements where the impact of the breach is negligible. The term "de minimis" is taken from a longer Latin phrase which translates into "the law does not concern itself with trifles." De minimis exceptions are commonly included in contracts to limit the application of covenants or other restrictions so that they do not apply in circumstances where the failure to observe the restriction has negligible impact. *Reference [21].*

**Deal flow:** The number of transactions that have closed or are expected to close during a given period. *Reference [1].*

**Debt & Cash-free pricing:** The target company's price without financial debts or cash. *Reference [1].*

**Debt financing:** Debt financing occurs when a firm raises money for working capital or capital expenditures by selling debt instruments to individuals and/or institutional investors. It is the opposite of equity financing, which entails issuing stock to raise money. *Reference [22].*

**Debt pushdown:** When the acquisition debt is transferred to the operating company rather than the company that generates the operating cash flow, if such a distinction exists. *Reference [1].*

**Debt redemption:** Lenders expect debt to be paid back by a date certain, the maturity date. The debt issuer - a governmental entity or corporation - redeems the debt upon maturity by paying the face value and any remaining interest due. After redemption, the debt has no value and pays no more interest. In some situations, an issuer may redeem debt before maturity. *Reference [23].*

**Disbursement:** The capital investors give to companies. *Reference [1].*

**Discount rate:** Interest rate or cost of opportunity used to calculate the present value of future cash flows. *Reference [24] adapted by authors.*

**Distressed investment:** An investment made into a company experiencing liquidity, capitalization and/or underperformance issues. *Reference [1].*

**Distribution:** The capital Limited Partners receive from General Partners after they exit an investment. *Reference [1].*

**Divestment:** Divesting is the opposite of investing. Divesting is the process of selling an asset and is done for either financial or social goals. The term is often used in a business context to describe companies or governments that divest some of their holdings by selling them off. Divesting is also known as divestiture and divestment. *Reference [25].*

**Downside protection:** Search Funds have evolved over the years to incorporate a downside protection strategy, primarily through the acquisition of healthy, stable companies that meet certain standardized criteria such as: established and profitable operation, strong cash flows, defensible market position, low CapEx requirements, operating in a fragmented industry, scalable and non-cyclical, just to mention a few. *Reference authors.*

**DPI (Distributed to Paid In):** The value of all distributions divided by the amount limited partners have contributed to the fund. *Reference [1].*

**Drag-along and Tag-along:** Drag-along rights are provisions that make it mandatory for a minority shareholder to agree and join the majority shareholders in the sale of a firm. In essence, the minority shareholder is "dragged along" in the sale process by the majority shareholders. This remains the case so long as the majority shareholders offer the minority shareholder the same terms and conditions as would any other seller. A drag-along right would normally form a section of a buy-sell agreement or unanimous shareholders' agreement between the stockholders of a company. Tag-along rights (or Rights of Co-Sale) is a minority shareholder protection affording the right to include their shares in any sale of control and at the offered price. *References [26, 27, 28].*

**Drawdown rate:** The speed at which a general partner calls down the capital committed by its limited partners. *Reference [1].*

**Dry Powder:** In Private Equity, Venture Capital and Search Funds, dry powder refers to the amount of cash still available for further investments or acquisitions. It is also an informal term that refers to highly liquid securities, cash reserves and any other security that can be converted to cash right away to meet debt obligations, cover operational expenses, or invest in opportunities. Having a lot of these liquid assets on hand gives organizations a financial advantage over others who do not and also plays an important role in credit. In context of M&A, dry powder means the amount of capital that is available to financial or strategic buyers for investment in strategic acquisitions, portfolio companies or add-on acquisitions. Also known as Capital Overhang. *Reference [29] adapted by authors.*

**Dual track:** A dual track strategy involve pursuing an IPO while simultaneously exploring the sale of portfolio companies through a private auction. *Reference [30].*

**Due diligence:** The process of analyzing and assessing individuals, companies, and investors before engaging in an acquisition. In Search Funds, the initial Search Capital is enough to usually cover up to 3 Due Diligences on target companies. *Reference [1].*

# E

**Early stage:** The period of investment between seed and late-stage deals, when companies already have a proven concept but relatively small revenues. *Reference [1].*

**Earn-out:** An earn-out is a financing arrangement for the purchase of a business in which the seller finances a portion of the purchase price, and payment of this amount is contingent on achieving a predetermined level of future earnings. An earn-out is often used to bridge a valuation gap. The seller only gets paid if the predetermined level of future EBITDA or other financial targets are achieved. *Reference [31].*

**Earn-out provision:** Part of a contract that details future compensation for the seller if the business attains certain performance goals. *Reference [1].*

**EBITDA (Earnings Before Interest, Taxes, Depreciation and Amortization):** A company's net profit plus interest, taxes, depreciation, and amortization. *Reference [1].*

**Emerging Economies:** The term was coined by Antoine van Agtmael in 1981 while working for the International Finance Corporation (IFC), a division of the World Bank. Agtmael wanted the term to evoke "progress, uplift and dynamism". An Emerging Economy is the economy of a developing nation that is becoming more engaged with global markets as it grows. Countries classified as Emerging Economies are those with some, but not all, of the characteristics of a developed market. As an Emerging Economy progresses it typically becomes more integrated with the global economy, as shown by increased liquidity in local debt and equity markets, increased trade volume and foreign direct investment, and the domestic development of modern financial and regulatory institutions. Currently, some notable emerging economies include Brazil, China, India, Mexico, Russia, and South Africa. Critically, an Emerging Economy is transitioning from a low income, less developed, often pre-industrial economy towards a modern, industrial economy with a higher standard of living. Although the term Emerging Economy is loosely defined, countries, varying in size, that fall into this category are usually considered emerging because of their unbalanced levels of development and reforms towards "freerer" trade. *References [32, 33].*

**Encumbrances:** An encumbrance is a legal claim on a property by a party that is not the owner. The term covers a wide range of financial and non-financial claims on a property by parties other than the titleholder. A mortgage is an obvious encumbrance; if a homeowner doesn't keep up with mortgage payments, the lender has the right to foreclose on the property. Any lien or claim on a property is an encumbrance. Zoning laws and environmental restrictions are also examples of encumbrances. The most common types of encumbrances apply to real estate. *References [34, 35].*

**Entrepreneurship:** Entrepreneurship is the implementation of a new or significantly improved good, service or process, a new marketing method or a new organizational method in business practices, workplace organization or external relations. *References [36, 37].*

**Entrepreneurship through Acquisition:** Acquiring and operating an existing established small business is a time-tested path to entrepreneurship. Rather than creating a new venture from scratch, the entrepreneur can search for an existing business – which has people, products, clients, suppliers, and processes – acquire and growth it. It includes the acquisition of traditional life style businesses, franchising, licensing, and each and every day more often also different kinds of Search Funds. *Reference [38].*

**EOS Entrepreneurial Operating System:** The Entrepreneurial Operating System (EOS) is a comprehensive business management philosophy designed specifically for entrepreneurial organizations to help them achieve greater operational efficiency and business success. It focuses on strengthening six key components of a business: Vision, People, Data, Issues, Process, and Traction. EOS aims to align the entire organization around a clear vision, ensure that the right people are in the right roles, use data to guide decision-making, systematically address issues, streamline processes to ensure consistency and scalability, and gain traction by executing well-defined goals. The system, popularized by Gino Wickman in his book "Traction", provides a set of simple concepts and practical tools that leaders and managers in growth-oriented businesses can use to get more out of their organizations and ensure that everyone is working effectively towards a common goal. *Reference authors.*

**Equity:** Capital that is invested in a company to buy shares and support growth or value creation. *Reference [39] adapted by authors.*

**Equity Gap:** Capital needed to conclude an acquisition by a Search Fund. Typically, in Search Funds, some investors that supported the Search by investing in the Search Capital will not participate in the Acquisition Capital, opening up space for new investors to participate through **Equity Gaps**. *Reference authors.*

**Equity Gap Notice and Equity Gap Term:** In the event that some of the transaction financing remains unsubscribed due to one or more Investors not contributing to their respective Pro-Rata Rights (in whole or in part) the resulting **Equity Gap** shall be filled respecting the following procedure: Purchasing Investors whose desired amount indicated in the Investor's Position Notice is higher than their Pro-Rata Right may fill the Equity Gap in accordance with their respective Pro-Rata Rights, calculated on the basis of the Securities held by the Purchasing Investor, should the Equity Gap be oversubscribed in any way. If the Equity Gap remains to be filled, the Searchers shall submit a written **Equity Gap Notice** to each Purchasing Investor, notifying the existence of the **Equity Gap** and offering the possibility to fill the remaining **Equity Gap**, by changing their Desired Amount within 5 to 10 business days from receiving the written **Equity Gap Term** from the Searchers. Upon notification of the **Equity Gap Notice** and until the Equity Gap is filled, the Searchers shall be free to offer the remaining amount to any Third Party, including investment funds, family offices, banks, or other financial institutions, for the purpose of duly completing the Transaction Financing. *Reference authors.*

**Equity Value:** Value of a company to the shareholders. It is the Enterprise Value (EV) plus all cash and cash equivalents, short and long-term investments, and less all short-term debt, long-term debt, and minority interests. *Reference [40].*

**Escrow Account or Holdback Account:** Escrow is the use of a third party, which holds an asset or funds before they are transferred from one party to another. This third-party holds the funds until both parties have fulfilled their contractual requirements. Also known as Holdback Account, is a portion of the purchase price that is not paid at the closing date. Sometimes Holdbacks relate to achieving a specific working capital threshold or in the event there is litigation outstanding at closing. *References [41, 42].*

**ESG (Environmental, Social and Governance):** Environmental, Social and Governance aspects of a business refers to the degree of sustainability of its operations. The concept is increasingly used by investors willing to invest in assets that comply with positive impact to society. *Reference [43].*

**EV (Enterprise Value):** A company's value calculated as market capitalization, including all debt and equity interests, minus excess cash. *Reference [1].*

**Evergreen fund:** A fund that never closes and keeps fundraising to ensure consistent cash flows. *Reference [1].*

**Exit:** When an investor sells its equity in a portfolio company. The last phase of a typical Search Fund cycle. *Reference [1].*

# F

**Family Office:** A firm that manages assets, investments, and trusts for a wealthy family. Family Offices of entrepreneurial families tend to support Search Funds or Funds of Funds investing in Search Funds. *Reference [1].*

**Final close:** When a General Partner stops fundraising. *Reference [1].*

**First Equity Gap Notice and First Equity Gap Term** (see **Equity Gap Notice** and **Equity Gap Term**).

**First-time fund:** Asset manager's first Private Equity (PE) vehicle. *Reference [44].*

**Fund:** An investment vehicle made by General Partners for Limited Partners. Limited Partners commit capital to funds and General Partners invest the capital into assets. *Reference [1].*

**Fund-of-funds:** A fund that invests in other funds. A fund-of-funds devotes all its time to evaluating fund managers, which usually leads to above-average returns. However, usually there are extra fees associated with investing in a fund-of-funds because investors pay the fees of the fund-of-funds that pay the fees of the funds. In Search Funds, most institutional funds can be considered funds-of-funds because the Search Fund is itself an investment vehicle. *Reference [1] adapted by authors.*

**Funding gap:** Capital needed to offset a cash flow shortage in a such specific period of time. *Reference [45] adapted by authors.*

**Fundraising:** In Private Equity or Venture Capital when General Partners ask for capital commitments from Limited Partners. In Search Funds, when Searchers ask for capital commitments from Search Fund investors for Search Capital or Acquisition Capital. *Reference [1].*

# G

**GDP (Gross Domestic Product):** Is the total monetary or market value of all the finished goods and services produced within a country's borders in a specific time period. *Reference [46].*

**Go-Shop Clause:** Clause that lets the seller actively solicit bids from other buyers – this term might be used as a compromise if the seller does not get exactly the price it is looking for. It is also used to reduce the risk of potential lawsuits if there was not a real "market check" before the deal was announced. *Reference [47].*

**Goodwill:** Accounting concept that evidences the willingness to pay a higher value for a particular asset. *Reference [48] adapted by authors.*

**GP (General Partner):** An entity that raises capital from limited partners for a fund and determines which assets the fund should invest in. *Reference [1].*

**Greenfield:** An investment that involves an asset or structure that does not yet exist. Investors fund all stages of development, including design, construction, infrastructure, and operations. In Search Funds, greenfields are markets with no or very little Search Fund or early-growth Private Equity deals. *Reference [1].*

**Growth equity investment:** When an investor gives a mature company capital it can use to expand or restructure in exchange for equity (usually a minority stake). *Reference [1].*

# H

**Hard Cap:** The maximum fund size that is stated in a Limited Partnership agreement by the General Partner. It represents the maximum General Partners reasonably believes they can invest over the fund's lifetime (maximum fund size). Typically, a Cap cannot be exceeded except by amendment of a partnership agreement. Limited partners generally disfavor increasing caps without an operational justification for doing so (e.g., if the fund wanted to add a principal), otherwise the investors fear that managers are simply taking advantage of the interest in the fund to enrich themselves on management fees from a larger fund and that they will be pressured into making larger and overpriced investments in order to put all the additional capital to work. *Reference [49] adapted by authors.*

**Headwind (see also Tailwind):** In the context of Search Funds, the term "headwind" is borrowed from aviation and meteorology to metaphorically describe factors or trends that makes growth, operations, or profitability more difficult for a company. These might include economic downturns, increased competition, regulatory changes, supply chain disruptions, or technological changes that negatively affect the business. For a Search Fund, identifying potential headwinds before acquiring a company is crucial, as they can significantly impact the investment's return. *Reference authors.*

**Heads of agreement:** The basic elements of a deal spelled out more specifically in a share purchase agreement. *Reference [1].*

**HHI (Herfindahl-Hirschman Index):** A commonly accepted way to measure concentration within an industry, which the US Department of Justice uses to review deals for anti-trust considerations. It is calculated by finding the square of the market share for each firm competing in a market and adding up the results, which can range from near zero to 10,000. *Reference [1].*

**Hurdle:** Minimum rate of return on an investment required by an investor. In Search Funds, hurdles are used to calculate the last trench of equity to the searcher CEO. *Reference [50] adapted by authors.*

# I

**Incubated Search:** It is a committed fund of capital for both the search and the acquisition that incubates, prepares, and helps Searchers on their paths, through providing mentorship and infrastructure, especially in the Searching Stage. *Reference [19] adapted by authors.*

**Incubator** (*see also* **Accelerator**)**:** An organization that gives early-stage companies office space, resources, advice, and networking opportunities (usually in exchange for equity). The primary difference is that Search Fund incubators focus solely on Search Funds, as opposed to a Private Equity firm that firms work with older executives with experience in an industry and generally looking at acquiring bigger companies. Typically, few entrepreneurs search from an incubator at the same time. *Reference [19] adapted by authors.*

**Institutional investor:** An entity that invests capital on the behalf of organizations, companies, or individuals. Examples include university endowments, insurance companies and pension funds. *Reference [1].*

**Investment bank:** A financial institution that serves as an agent or underwriter for security issuances. Some investment banks also act as brokers/dealers and provide advisory services for mergers, acquisitions, restructurings, and other transactions. *Reference [1].*

**Investor's Position Notice** (see **Equity Gap Notice**).

**IPO (Initial Public Offering):** The first time a private company's stock is available to the public. All companies undergoing an IPO must register with the American SEC (Securities and Exchange Commission) or similar in another country and take the necessary steps to comply with all applicable rules and regulations of a publicly traded company. *Reference [1].*

**IRR (Internal Rate of Return):** The rate at which the net present value of all cash flows from an investment will equal zero. IRR is commonly used to measure the performance of a fund. *Reference [1].*

# J

**J curve:** The expression can be used to illustrate the Search Fund journey. During the Search Fund journey the initial investment phase (descending part of the J) can include the Search and the Acquisition Capital used to start the process, the transition phase (the bottom of the J) involves making strategic and operational improvements in the acquired company and the growth and profitability followed by the exit (ascending Part of the J) is where the majority of the financial gains are realized, potentially leading to a significant spike in returns. *Reference [1] adapted by authors.*

# K

**Key-person clause (Key-man clause or Key-man provision):** Contractual clause that prohibits the fund manager or General Partner from making key investments if one or more named key principals fail to devote a specific amount of time to the partnership. The general partner or fund manager can restart investments only after new replacement key executives are appointed and approved by the partners of a limited partnership firm. The only exception to this rule is the investments that have been agreed to before the key-man clause took place. *Reference [51].*

**KPI (Key Performance Indicator):** A set of metrics used to gauge the performance of a company. KPIs depend on a specific company's strategic and operational goals. Examples include revenue growth and monthly active users. *Reference [1].*

# L

**Late stage:** The final period of Venture Capital investment (usually after Series C), when Startups have increased revenue and are near exit. *Reference [1].*

**LBO (Leveraged Buyout):** Acquisition of another company using a significant amount of borrowed money (bonds or loans) to meet the cost of acquisition. *Reference [52].*

**Lead or Anchor investor:** The investor that makes the largest investment in a fund. As the primary financier of the round, the lead investor can have specific benefits like better fees or better service. *Reference [1] adapted by authors.*

**Leakage:** Term used to refer to extractions of value by the seller, such as dividends during the post- locked box period (unless mutually agreed). Such items diminish the balance sheet value in the period between locked box and completion which, if unadjusted, would mean the buyer receiving less value than they have paid for. The buyer will typically receive protection via the SPA against leakage. *Reference [18].*

**Leaver provisions:** Compulsory transfer clauses that are included in a shareholder's agreement (SHA) to ensure that on departure the leaving director or employee must transfer his shares, for an agreed value, back to the other shareholders or to the company. *Reference [53].*

**Legal continuity:** The question of whether the target company's existing contracts should be retained after an acquisition. In asset deals, prior agreements typically cease and must be entered into again. Legal continuity rarely impacts share deals. *Reference [1].*

**Leverage:** The use of debt in an investment, including acquisitions and capital expenditures. With leverage, general partners can expedite improvements to portfolio companies and amplify returns. *Reference [1].*

**Leveraged recapitalization:** Corporate finance transaction in which a company changes its capitalization structure by replacing the majority of its equity with a package of debt securities consisting of both senior bank debt and subordinated debt. A leveraged recapitalization is also referred to as leveraged recap. *Reference [54].*

**Limited Partnership:** The most common form of business organization used by Private Equity funds. The organization created is comprised of a General Partner, who manages the fund, and Limited Partners, who invest money but have limited liability and are not involved with the day-to-day management of the fund. In the typical Private Equity fund, the General Partner receives a management fee and a percentage of the profits (known as performance fee or carried interest). The Limited Partners receive income, capital gains, and tax benefits. *Reference [9].*

**Liquidation:** The process of selling assets in order to pay creditors (and potentially shareholders). *Reference [1].*

**Liquidity event:** When a general partner sells equity in an asset and returns capital to its Limited Partners. *Reference [1].*

**Lock-up period:** Contractual provision preventing insiders of a company from selling their shares for a specified period of time. Investment banks that underwrite initial public offerings (IPOs) generally insist upon lock-ups of at least 180 days from large shareholders (1% ownership or more) in order to allow an orderly market to develop in the shares. The shareholders that are subject to lock-up usually include the management and directors of the company, strategic partners, and such large investors. These shareholders have typically invested prior to the IPO at a significantly lower price to that offered to the public and therefore stand to gain considerable profits. If a shareholder attempts to sell shares that are subject to lock-up during the lock-up period, the transfer agent will not permit the sale to be completed. *Reference [9].*

**Locked Box Mechanism and Locked Box Date or Locked Box Day** (*see also* **Completion accounts**): It is how to deal with the value movement in the balance sheet due to trading between the Locked Box Date and the Date of Closing. From a Seller's perspective, they may still be managing the business to generate profit and will have capital tied up until the completion date when the consideration is paid. This adjustment is often referred to as the "value accrual". *Reference [18].*

**LOI (Letter of Intent):** The initial document that outlines the goals of the parties involved in a deal and is drafted to open negotiations under clauses dictating exclusivity and secrecy. A LOI is sometimes called a memorandum of understanding (MOU). In Search Funds, LOIs are important indicators of performance during the Search phase. *Reference [1] adapted by authors.*

**LP (Limited Partner):** An entity that commits capital to a General Partner's fund. LPs are the investors into private equity funds which are managed by a General Partner (GP). In a limited partnership, the limited partners are merely investors with no responsibility for managing the business of the partnership. In fact, to preserve their limited liability (similar to shareholders in a corporation), the Limited Partners are actually not allowed to manage the business of the partnership. Limited Partners are not involved in the day-to-day management of the partnership and generally cannot lose more than their capital contribution. *References [1, 55, 9, 56].*

# M

**MAC (Material Adverse Change):** Is a change in circumstances that significantly reduces the value of a company. For an LOI to become a share purchase agreement, usually the basic circumstances at the target company cannot change. *Reference [1] adapted by authors.*

**MAE (Material Adverse Effect):** These clauses give the buyer an "out" if something catastrophic happens between signing the agreement and closing the deal. *Reference [47].*

**Management fee:** The amount General Partners charge Limited Partners to operate a fund. The fee is usually between 0.5% and 3% of the called capital amount. *Reference [1].*

**MBA (Master in Business Administration):** Graduate degree program that combines theoretical and practical training for business or investment management. MBA programs typically include core classes in accounting, management, finance, marketing, and business law. Management training is at the heart of any MBA curriculum, with a focus on leadership, planning, business strategy, organizational behavior, and the more human sides of running a large or small business. *Reference [94] adapted by authors.*

**MBI (Management Buy-In):** It occurs when a management team buys an outside company and replaces the company's directors, managers, and leadership. Usually, this replacement is driven by a poorly management situation. *Reference [57] adapted by authors.*

**MBO (Management Buy-Out):** It occurs when a management team buys a company they are associated with and then leads the operation. *Reference [1].*

**M&A (Mergers & Acquisitions):** Consolidation of companies or assets through various types of financial transactions like mergers, acquisitions, tender offers, purchase of assets, and management acquisitions. *Reference [1].*

**Mezzanine Debt:** Word of Italian origin that refers to a middle portion of architecture (often a structure in between two floors). When it comes to finance, the term refers to financing that is halfway between equity (stocks) and senior debt (senior bonds). Mezzanine loans are debt, just like bonds. They are junior to most bonds, which means that in the event of a bankruptcy, the bondholders get paid back first, then mezzanine investors, then owners of stock. Unlike bonds, mezzanine debt can be traded like a stock. This makes it more liquid as well as riskier. In Search Funds, it might take place when one or more of the acquisition investors need more time to transfer the money for international acquisitions and they use local Mezzanine Debt to conclude the deal. *Reference [58]*.

**Mezzanine investment:** A financing round between senior and subordinated loans that typically includes equity-based options in the form of warrants. *Reference [1]*.

**Micro Private Equity:** Micro Private Equity refers to organized pools of capital used in the acquisition of businesses under $5 million in enterprise value. Traditional Private Equity and Search Funds will usually not acquire businesses below this valuation level due to the lack of systems and sophisticated management generally associated with businesses of this size. Micro Private Equity are typically not structured as a formalized fund, but, rather, a group of high-net-worth individuals that will invest on a deal-by-deal basis. In Emerging Economies, however, Search Funds can acquire relatively sophisticated business under $5 million in enterprise value. *Reference [59]*.

**Middle-market company:** Term used in Private Equity to refer to companies with an enterprise value of $25M–$1B. *Reference [1].*

**Monitoring fees:** Monitoring fees are the fees charged by a Private Equity firm to its portfolio companies for ongoing advisory and management services after the acquisition. Expenses are typically reimbursed separately. In each transaction covered by this survey, the controlling stockholder charged an annual monitoring fee in cash under an agreement entered into at the time of the acquisition. The nature of the advisory and management services is usually described in detail, but with no specific level or amount of services being required to earn the monitoring fee. Monitoring fees can be charged as a fixed amount in cash or as a percentage of EBITDA of the target company (usually in between 1% and 3%). *Reference [60] adapted by authors.*

**Multiple arbitrage:** The investment gains achieved by increasing the sales multiple relative to the original investment multiple. For example, buying a company at 4x EBITDA and selling it at 7x EBITDA. *Reference [1].*

**Mutatis mutandis:** Medieval Latin expression meaning "with things changed that should be changed" or "once the necessary changes have been made". It is used in contracts like Shareholders Agreements (SHA) to acknowledge that a comparison being made requires certain obvious alterations, which are left unstated. It is not to be confused with the similar *ceteris paribus*, which excludes any changes other than those explicitly mentioned. *Reference authors.*

# N

**NAV (Net Asset Value):** The Net Asset Value (NAV) represents a fund's per share market value. It is frequently used by fund of funds investing in Search Funds and is calculated by dividing the total value of all the cash and securities in a fund's portfolio, minus any liabilities, by the number of outstanding shares. The NAV calculation is important because it shows how much one share of the fund is worth. *Reference [61].*

**NDA (Non-disclosure agreement):** A pact between the parties involved in a deal that confirms they will not misuse the information exchanged during negotiations. *Reference [1].*

**Net Debt:** There is no universal definition of Net Debt, which makes its definition in a LOI and SPA paramount. Typically, Net Debt includes cash less financial liabilities (loans, bills of exchange, repayable subsidies, pensions and other long-term commitments to staff, commissions giving rise to cash outflows within the foreseeable future, off-balance sheet commitments that can be considered equivalent to debt and certain leasing debts). *Reference [1].*

**No-aggravation:** It is a measure to prevent different parties to worsening the negotiable or commercial conditions within a dispute process. Usually intermediate by an arbitrage chamber. *References [62, 63].*

**No-shop Clause:** A buyer who would like to avoid being out-bid by other potential acquirers, so it's in their interest to include a "no-shop" clause that says the company may not consider alternative offers. *Reference [47].*

**Normalized working capital:** An analysis of a target company that accounts for all one-off or non-recurring items to determine how working capital normally operates. *Reference [1].*

# O

**Offer letter:** A non-binding indication of one party's intention to purchase a target company. *Reference [1].*

**Onkochishin:** Japanese expression meaning "understand the past to see a future based on it". The expression, commonly used in Private Equity, explains how value can be created after the acquisition of a company with high potential to grow. *Reference [64].*

**Operating partner:** An executive dedicated to working with portfolio companies to increase their value. They often have an expertise in a certain area (like a specific industry). *Reference [1].*

**Operating phase:** Stage of which the searcher CEO manages the acquired company aiming to grow the business. *Reference [65].*

**OTC (Over-the-Counter):** Over-the-counter (OTC) refers to the process of how securities are traded via a brokers or dealers as opposed to on a centralized exchange. Over-the-counter trading can involve equities, debt instruments, and derivatives, which are financial contracts that derive their value from an underlying asset such as a commodity. *Reference [66] adapted by authors.*

**Owner or Founder:** Executive that controls the company before being acquired by a Search Fund. *Reference [19] adapted by authors.*

**Ownership:** Becoming full or partial owner of a company's stake share. Ownership of the company is determined by who owns the shares, and battles for ownership may take place when a person or entity acquires a sufficient number of shares to seek one or more seats on the company's board of directors. *Reference [67].*

# P

**P to P Transactions (Public-to-Private):** A public-to-private transaction involves the acquisition by a private-equity-backed vehicle of a public target company (which we will refer to as 'P2P Target'), and as a result combines the features of a traditional private company management buyout with the structural and regulatory requirements of a public company takeover. It is also often referred to as a 'take private' transaction *Reference [68]*.

**Paid-in capital:** The amount of committed capital that has been transferred from the Limited Partner to the General Partner. *Reference [1]*.

**Payout:** It is a metric that states the proportion of profits distribution to the shareholders. *Reference [69] adapted by authors*.

**Permitted leakage** (*see also* **Locked Box Mechanism**): The intention of permitted leakage is to carve-out certain items from the leakage protection. The seller will undertake not to extract value from the business except for items specifically agreed between the parties and clearly defined in the SPA. *Reference [18]*.

**Permitted transfers:** Is the allowed transfer of a right, asset or security from one party to another. The transferee is usually a subsidiary, or an entity controlled by or under the same control of the transferor. Therefore, the transfer does not trigger certain shareholder's rights such as tag-along, co-sale rights, right of first option or refusal. *Reference authors.*

**PIPE (Private Investment in Public Equity):** When a private investor purchases stock in a public company (usually for less than the current market price). *Reference [1].*

**Placement agent:** A third-party firm that helps General Partners fundraise. *Reference [1].*

**Platform company:** A Private Equity-backed company that completes an add-on transaction. *Reference [1].*

**Pledge fund:** A pledge fund is a type of investment vehicle in which the participants agree (or "pledge") to contribute capital to a series of investments at the time of each investment opportunity. Contributors to a Pledge fund reserve the right to review each investment prior to contributing. A Pledge fund is a Private Equity solution for GPs aiming to locate a specific investment opportunity (for example, a company for acquisition) before presenting it to LPs. The main difference between a Private Equity Pledge fund and a Search Fund consists in the role of the Searcher who leads the process in an entrepreneurial manner, instead of managing it from an investment banking manner. *Reference [92] adapted by authors.*

**Portfolio company:** A company that has received an investment from a Private Equity, Venture Capital, or Search Fund Investment firm. *Reference [1].*

**Post-money valuation:** The value of a company after an infusion of capital. *Reference [1].*

**PPM (Private Placement Memorandum):** The "Business Plan" of Search Funds. It is a detailed and standardized document where the Searchers state the terms and conditions of the investment opportunity for potential investors. *Reference [65].*

**Pre-money valuation:** The value of a company investors determines before they invest capital. *Reference [1].*

**Pre-seed:** The stage before the seed stage. As seed-stage investing has become more popular, investors have started to invest in companies at this stage in the hopes of finding them early on. A pre-seed company is often just the founder(s) and an idea. *Reference [1].*

**Private Equitization of Capitalism:** The ongoing process of transforming the equity (stocks) of all kinds of limited companies, including SMEs, into a commodity. This process is enhanced by globalization and by the spread and automatization of knowledge on mergers and acquisitions (M&A). It started via Private Equity in the 1980's and is spreading fast throughout the world since the 2010's. *Reference authors.*

**Private Equity:** Kind of Capital that is not noted on the public stock exchange. Private Equity involves investors giving private companies capital in exchange for equity. *Reference [1].*

**Public market equivalent:** An analysis that compares a Private Equity fund's performance to a public benchmark or index. *Reference [1].*

**Public-to-private transaction:** When a Private Equity firm acquires all the shares of a public company, changing the company's status from public to private. *Reference [1].*

**Put Option and Put Option Notice:** A Put Option is a right (but not an obligation) for its owner to sell a specified number of shares or securities at a specified price for a fixed or indefinite period. The holder of the Put Option right exercises his or her rights by means of a Put Option Notice generally to the issuer of the shares or securities. *Reference authors.*

# R

**Ratchet:** A ratchet is an anti-dilution protection mechanism whereby management's equity stake may be altered on the happening of various future events. It is provided as an incentive to management, as they are given the opportunity to achieve additional economic compensation. *Reference [70].*

**Recapitalization:** An investment strategy that involves restructuring a company's debt and equity mixture. *Reference [1].*

**Releverage:** Refers to the process of increasing the level of debt in the capital structure of the acquired company after an initial period of deleveraging or stabilization. During the acquisition searchers and investors tend to use a significant amount of debt or seller notes to acquire a company. Post-acquisition, the focus is often on reducing this debt, either through operational improvements that generate cash flow or through asset sales. After the company pays down its debt, the searcher CEO and his or her board may choose to releverage the company, taking on additional debt, which can be used for various purposes such as funding new growth initiatives, paying dividends to shareholders, or financing additional acquisitions. Releveraging is often done when the company is in a stronger financial position and can handle additional debt without significant risk. The decision to releverage must be carefully considered, as it increases the company's financial risk. The additional debt can put pressure on the company's cash flows and may make it more vulnerable to economic downturns. However, if managed properly, releveraging can enhance equity returns (through financial leverage) and facilitate further growth or value creation within the company. In some cases, a searcher CEOs and investors might use a releveraging strategy as part of preparing a company for sale. By increasing the debt, they can extract value in the form of dividends, thereby realizing some return on their investment prior to the actual sale of the company. Reference authors.

**Reverse Merger, Reverse Takeover or Reverse IPO:** Typically occur through a simpler, shorter, and less expensive process than a conventional IPO. In a reverse merger, investors of the private company acquire a majority of the shares of a public shell company, which is then combined with the purchasing entity. Investment banks and financial institutions typically use shell companies as vehicles to complete these deals. These simple shell companies can be registered with the Securities and Exchange Commission (SEC) on the front end (prior to the deal), making the registration process relatively straightforward and less expensive. To consummate the deal, the private company trades shares with the public shell in exchange for the shell's stock, transforming the acquirer into a public company. *Reference [71].*

**Reverse termination fee:** A fee paid by the buyer if it breaches or decides to terminate a definitive acquisition agreement. *Reference [1].*

**Ride the cycle:** When a company grow together with a local economic or sector growth. The investment made in this company is directly benefited by the cycle. *Reference authors.*

**ROI (Return on investment):** The percentage of profit or loss that resulted from an investment. *Reference [1].*

**Rolled Equity:** Term used to describe the receipt of shares from the buyer as full or partial consideration for the acquisition. It usually occurs between private company sellers and buyers and is most often utilized by Private Equity firms and their platform or portfolio companies. The equity isn't actually the same equity, but rather the component of the total purchase price that the seller receives in the form of the buyer's stock as part of the sale proceeds. *Reference [72].*

**Rollover Equity:** It happens when certain equity holders in the acquired company, including founders, and key members of the management team, roll a portion of their ownership stake over into the new equity capital structure put in place by the acquiring Search Fund in lieu of receiving cash proceeds. This kind of arrangement is attractive to Private Equity investors because it reduces their cash outlay and also helps align investor and management team objectives, as the latter will continue to have "skin in the game" post-acquisition. However, the arrangement is avoided in Search Funds as searchers now converted in CEOs and their investors need complete freedom and control to change and improve the acquired company. The arrangement might look appealing to those sellers rolling their equity because it allows them to receive partial liquidity for their investment and still participate in further upside. Also, rolling equity may be attractive to the sellers from a tax perspective. *Reference [73], adapted by the authors.*

**RSU (Restricted Stock Unit):** Refers to a form of compensation issued by an employer to an employee in the form of company shares. Restricted stock units are issued to employees through a vesting plan and distribution schedule after they achieve required performance milestones or upon remaining with their employer for a particular length of time. *Reference [74].*

**Rule of 40:** Companies that have combined revenue growth and EBITDA margin equal or above 40%. Usually, these are healthy companies. The Rule of 40 is a high-level metric for software company success that has been getting more and more popular, especially in the realms of Venture Capital and growth equity. The success indicator is generally concerned with two very important KPIs for SaaS businesses, growth rate and profit margin. According to the Rule of 40, if the combination of a SaaS business' growth rate and profit margin is greater than 40%, the business is viable and on the right track to becoming a mature company. Sometimes, the Rule of 40 is applied to other service industries as well. *Reference authors.*

**RVPI (Residual Value to Paid In):** Also known as Net Asset Value (NAV) divided by Paid-In capital. The ratio of the current value of all remaining investments within a fund to the total contributions of Limited Partners to date. This ratio measures how much unrealized value remains in the investment. A RVPI ratio of 0.70x means that the remaining investments are valued at 70 cents for every dollar contributed. *Reference [75].*

# S

**SAFE (Simple Agreement for Future Equity):** An agreement between an investor and a company that provides rights to the investor for future equity in the company similar to a warrant, except without determining a specific price per share (or a valuation) at the time of the initial investment. *Reference [76].*

**Scale Ups:** Small or Medium size enterprise (SME) that has already validated its products and proved that its economics are profitable and sustainable, having an average annual growth positive for the last 3 to 5 years. *Reference authors.*

**Search Capital:** The Search Capital is used to cover a modest salary and administrative and deal-related expenses over a two-year period (or two-and-a-half year's period in Emerging Economies) while the entrepreneur searches full-time for an acquisition. *References [65, 2] adapted by authors.*

**Search Fund:** A growing kind of Entrepreneurship through Acquisition. The term "Search Fund" originated at Harvard Business School and Stanford Graduate School of Business in 1984 and has spread steadily to top business schools and entrepreneurs around the world. It is an investment vehicle, through which investors financially support an entrepreneur's efforts to locate, acquire, manage, and grow a privately held company. *References [65, 77].*

**Searcher:** Typically, it is one or two young talented individuals who form an investment vehicle named Search Fund with a group of aligned investors, in order to search for, acquire, and lead a privately held company for the medium to long term, typically six to ten years. *Reference [65].*

**Searcher CEO:** Searcher that turned out to become the CEO of its acquired company. *Reference [65].*

**Searching phase:** Search Fund life cycle stage when the searcher is looking for a company to acquire after successfully completed the fundraising of the Search Capital. *Reference [65].*

**Secondary Buy-Out:** It is the sale of a portfolio company by one financial sponsor or Private Equity fund to another. *Reference [78].*

**Secondary market:** When one Limited Partner sells its alternative investments to another Limited Partner. Limited Partners do this for a variety of reasons, including to adjust their asset allocation. In Search Funds, it happens when institutional investors sell their participation to third parties. *Reference [1] adapted by authors.*

**Second Equity Gap Notice and Second Equity Gap Term** (see **Equity Gap Notice** and **Equity Gap Term**).

**Seed Investment:** The first stage of Venture Capital investment, before early stage. *Reference [1].*

**Self-Funded Search Fund:** Search Fund financially backed by the Searcher up to the Acquisition stage, including or note Due Diligence costs, in order to get a higher stake (more equity than in Traditional Search Funds) on the acquired company. *Reference [19] adapted by authors.*

**Seller Notes or Vendor Financing:** A form of deferred payment. It can come with or without interest, depending on the terms that are most favorable to the vendor. It is extensively used in Private Equity and in Search Funds. In Emerging Economies, it is even more utilized as access to bank loans are generally limited. *Reference [79].*

**Senior debt:** The debt that takes priority over other securities in the event of liquidation. *Reference [1].*

**Series A to D or more:** The identification of Venture Capital investment rounds after Seed Capital investment. *Reference [1].*

**SHA (Shareholders Agreement):** It is a contract that stipulates obligations, rights, and protections between shareholders. This contract typically outlines agreements pertaining to company stock, shareholder protection, firm leadership, and management. *Reference [80].*

**Share deal:** When the shares of a target company are acquired. *Reference [1].*

**Single-Investor or Single-Sponsored Search Fund:** Search Fund financially backed by one or no more than 3 investors. *Reference authors.*

**Skin in the game:** Term used in Private Equity to refer to owners or GPs having a significant stake in an investment fund or vehicle. In this phrase, "skin" is a figure of speech for the time of the person or the amount of money involved in the investment, and "game" is the metaphor for actions on the field of play (investment fund, acquired company, etc). *Reference authors.*

**SME (Small and Medium Enterprise):** Businesses that maintain revenues, assets, or a number of employees below a certain threshold. Each country has its own definition of what constitutes an SME. These companies play a crucial role in the economy, employing vast numbers of people and helping to shape innovation. *Reference [81] adapted by authors.*

**Sovereign wealth fund:** A state-owned investment fund designed to protect and/or grow a range of financial assets, including stocks, bonds, and natural resources. *Reference [1].*

**SPA (Share purchase agreement):** The final contract between parties involved in a deal that is subject to a number of condition precedents determined during negotiations. *Reference [1].*

**SPAC (Special Purpose Acquisition Company):** Special Purpose Acquisition Company is a vehicle formed to raise an amount of capital through an initial public offering (IPO) or the purpose of acquiring or merging with an existing company. Although conceptually similar, SPACs differ a lot from the Search Funds on the investment thesis: acquisition size, CEO profile, pipeline of deals, stage of the companies, profile of companies and vehicles used, among others, are different. *Reference [82] adapted by authors.*

**Spin-in:** Occurs when a company (often a larger corporation) spins in a business, technology, or product that was initially developed outside of its corporate structure, usually by a smaller, independent entity such as a Startup or a small business. *Reference authors.*

**Spin-off (***see also* **Carve-out):** A type of divestiture that creates an independent company through the sale or distribution of new shares of an existing business or division of a company. *Reference [1].*

**Staple financing:** A pre-arranged financing package offered to potential acquirers that includes all the details of a lending package. The name comes from the fact that the financing details are stapled to the back of the acquisition Term Sheet. *Reference [1].*

**Step up:** Upon Transaction and subject to contribution to the Transaction Financing (see **Acquisition Capital**), the Purchasing Investors will be ensured to have securities in the acquisition vehicle with a value equal to 150% of the total contributions made by each Purchasing Investor during the Search Period (see **Search Capital**). *Reference authors.*

**Step up multiple:** The difference between the post-valuation of a company's previous Venture Capital round and the pre-money valuation of its new round. *Reference [1].*

**Strategic acquisition:** When a corporation acquire a company (often a competitor) for its technology, products, services, employees, brand recognition, client base or base of suppliers. *Reference [1] adapted by authors.*

**Subordinated debt:** Loans that have a lower priority than senior debt in the event of liquidation. *Reference [1].*

**Succession:** Stage of transferring the leadership, role, power, shares, assets, among other benefits to third parties or to a new generation of executives. Generally, it comes when the founders achieve a certain age or stage of their careers and wants to step out to the organization. *Reference [83] adapted by authors.*

**Sweet Equity:** It is a type of financial instrument that represents any form of non-monetary equity that the owners or employees of a business contribute to the venture. Sweet equity can come in the form of options, rights, warrants, restricted stocks and RSUs or other forms of equity. *Reference [84].*

# T

**Tag-Along** (*see* **Drag-along and Tag-along**).

**Tailwind (see also Headwind):** In the context of Search Funds, the term "tailwind" is borrowed from aviation and meteorology to metaphorically describe factors that can help the performance and growth of a business. It refers to factors or trends that positively impact a business, propelling it forward more easily, just like a tailwind in aviation helps an airplane move faster. Tailwinds might include favorable market trends, technological advancements that benefit the business, regulatory changes that open up new opportunities, or macroeconomic factors that boost demand for the company's products or services. The ability to identify and react to these factors can significantly impact the success of the acquired company and, consequently, the return on investment for the fund's investors. *Reference authors.*

**Target company:** The entity purchased by an acquirer. *Reference [1].*

**Target working capital:** An amount recorded during negotiations to reflect a historical analysis of the working capital requirements of a target company. It reflects closing accounts as well as an increased or decreased price if a target company has more or less working capital than the target capital on the date of the closing accounts. *Reference [1].*

**Term sheet:** A term sheet is a bulleted list, prepared by any of the proposing parties, enumerating some of the features as well as the terms and conditions of a contemplated business agreement. The terms and conditions contained in this document are not binding to any of the parties, as they are subject to modification through further negotiations before the final agreement is actually prepared and signed. *Reference [85].*

**Toe-hold investing:** Refers to the strategy of acquiring a small initial stake or minority interest in a target company as a preliminary step towards a potential future acquisition. It involves making a relatively small investment to establish a presence and gain some level of influence or control in the target company. The purpose of toe-hold investing is often to monitor the company's performance, build a relationship with management, and gather information to assess the potential for a larger investment or acquisition in the future. Toe-hold investments can be a strategic approach to gradually increase ownership or negotiate favorable terms before committing to a full acquisition. *Reference authors.*

**Total Cap:** The term typically refers to the "Total Capitalization" of a company, representing the sum of a company's long-term debt, equity, and any other types of financing it uses. It essentially reflects the total value of all sources of capital used by the company. *Reference authors.*

**Traction (**see also **EOS Entrepreneurial Operating System):** Stage of accelerated growth and progress of a company, usually SMEs or Startups. Important stage of business consolidation. In Search Funds it might also refer to Gino Wickman's book "Traction" and its EOS Entrepreneurial Operating System often adopted by searcher CEOs. *Reference authors.*

**Trade sale (**see also **Strategic acquisition):** In Private Equity, refers to the sale of a portfolio company to another company operating in the same industry or a related field. This type of sale is a common exit strategy used by Private Equity firms to realize a return on their investment. *Reference authors.*

**Tranche:** A portion of an investment dependent on a company hitting certain milestones. Every tranche of a round is part of the same round. *Reference [1].*

**Transaction, One-Time, Deal or Success fees:** The amount Private Equity firms charge the companies they acquire (typically between 1% and 2%). Fees are charged by the Private Equity firm in connection with the completion of the acquisition for typically unspecified advisory services. Fees are collected in cash. *Reference [1].*

**TSA (Transition Services Agreements):** When a company is sold in an M&A transaction and the seller is expected to continue to provide services to support the post-closing company, the parties to the transaction enter into a transition services agreement (TSA), which governs the provision of such services to the post-closing company. *Reference [86].*

**Turnaround:** It is a restructuring process carried within a particular company or company's division in order to have an upward shift or improvement after it experienced a period of negative results. Search Funds traditionally do not acquire companies in need of a turnaround. *Reference [87] adapted by authors.*

**TVPI (Total Value to Paid In):** The value of all remaining investments in a fund plus the value of all distributions relative to the amount Limited Partners have contributed to the fund. *Reference [1].*

# U

**Underserved Acquisition Niche:** Refers to a segment of the market that is under-targeted or overlooked by larger Private Equity firms and corporate buyers. These are usually smaller, profitable businesses often led by retiring owners, typically with an EBITDA between $1 million to $5 million, which fall below the threshold of most private equity funds or larger acquirers. Search Funds aim to capitalize on these opportunities by identifying, acquiring, and operating such companies. These niches typically exist in fragmented industries, are geographically dispersed, and are often in sectors not considered "sexy" by typical Private Equity investors. By targeting these underserved acquisition niches, Search Fund entrepreneurs can take advantage of a lack of buyer competition and can often purchase these companies at more favorable multiples than in larger deals. *Reference authors.*

**Underwriting:** When investment banks issue debt and equity securities on behalf of corporations and governments to generate investment capital. *Reference [1].*

**Unicorn:** Usually is a Venture Capital-backed company with a valuation of $1 billion or more. The expression could be applied to other asset class portfolio companies like Search Funds. *Reference [1] adapted by authors.*

**Unlisted or Unquoted company:** An unlisted public company, also known as an unquoted public company, is a firm that has issued equity shares that are no longer traded on a stock exchange. Over-the-counter (OTC) markets that trade unlisted public companies typically have less transparency than public exchanges. *Reference [88] adapted by authors.*

**Upside potential:** Refers to the prospective gains or returns that investors could realize if the acquired company performs well. The term often relates to the growth potential of the companies located in the search phase and the possible exit strategies. If the searcher CEO successfully grows the acquired company, it could result in significant returns for the investors upon a successful exit, such as a sale to a strategic buyer, an initial public offering (IPO), or a recapitalization.

# V

**Value accrual** (*see* **Locked Box Mechanism**).

**Value Creation:** Value Creation is the process of turning labor and resources into something that meets the needs of others. Value creation is the goal of every successful business entity, creating value for customers helps you sell your products and services with ease. In the same vein, creating value for shareholders in the form of an increase in dividends and stock prices ensures the availability of investment capital to fund future operations. Fund managers and investors, together with the management of the company, apply their deep industry expertise to improve revenues, gain operational efficiency, retain talent or increase the bottom line before selling an upgraded company for a multiple higher than they were acquired for. *Reference authors.*

**Venture Capital:** A type of Private Equity investment that focuses on Startups and early-stage companies with long-term, high-growth potential. Usually, the high growth potential is based on innovations or new technologies. *Reference [1].*

**Vesting (provisions):** Right to receive a present or future payment, asset, or shares, among other benefits, usually conditioned to the achievement of milestones and/or minimum period of time. *Reference [89].*

**Vintage year:** When a fund closes and starts investing. In a series of funds, each fund is considered to have a vintage. The expression can also be used to refer to funds of the same type or funds established in the same year. *Reference [1] adapted by authors.*

# W

**WACC (Weighted Average Cost of Capital):** Represents a firm's average cost of capital from all sources, including common stock, preferred stock, bonds, and other forms of debt. The WACC tells us the return that lenders and shareholders expect to receive in return for providing capital to a company. For example, if lenders require a 10% return and shareholders require 20%, then a company's WACC is 15%. *Reference [90].*

**Warrant:** A security that gives the holder the option to purchase a company's stock at a predetermined price for a specified period. *Reference [1].*

**Waterfall Distribution:** The way in which the capital allocated to a Private Equity fund returns to both Limited Partners and General Partners. A waterfall structure can be pictured as a set of buckets or phases. Each bucket contains its own allocation method. When the bucket is full, the capital flows into the next bucket. The first buckets are usually entirely allocated to the Limited Partners, while buckets further away from the source are more advantageous to the General Partners. This structure is designed to encourage the General

Partner to maximize the return of the fund. *Reference [91] adapted by authors.*

**Working capital:** The customers, suppliers, inventories and other assets and liabilities required for day-to-day operations of a company. *Reference [1].*

# Z

**Zombie fund:** A fund that invests all its committed capital but holds onto investments longer than normal in expectation of a big exit or to continue collecting management fees. *Reference [1] adapted by authors.*

\*\*\*

# References

1. https://pitchbook.com/blog/private-equity-and-venture-capital-glossary
2. A Primer on Search Funds: A Practical Guide to Entrepreneurs Embarking on a Search Fund. Stanford Graduate School of Business. 2020.
3. Morrissette, S. G.; Hines, S. An Investor's Guide to Search Funds. The Journal of Private Equity. 2015.
4. https://www.investopedia.com/terms/a/amortization.asp
5. https://www.divestopedia.com/definition/5875/anti-embarrassment-clause
6. https://www.investopedia.com/terms/a/assetclasses.asp
7. https://www.divestopedia.com/definition/8387/binding-offer
8. https://www.divestopedia.com/definition/923/break-up-fee
9. https://ilpa.org/private-equity-glossary/
10. https://www.investopedia.com/terms/b/broker.asp
11. https://www.divestopedia.com/definition/4751/buy-and-build-strategy
12. https://www.investopedia.com/terms/c/cagr.asp

13. https://caia.org/
14. https://www.investopedia.com/terms/c/capitalexpenditure.asp
15. https://corporatefinanceinstitute.com/resources/templates/word-templates-transactions/cim-confidential-information-memorandum/
16. https://www.mayerbrown.com/en/perspectives-events/publications/2020/05/covid19-and-club-deals-an-alternative-to-debt-financing-for-acquirors
17. https://www.divestopedia.com/definition/927/club-deal
18. https://www.grantthornton.be/globalassets/1.-member-firms/belgium/insights/articles-and-blogs/completion-mechanisms---completion-accounts-or-locked-box.pdf
19. Dennis, J.; Laseca, E. The Evolution of Entrepreneurship Through Acquisition. The University of Chicago Booth School of Business. 2016.
20. https://www.divestopedia.com/definition/753/data-room
21. https://uk.practicallaw.thomsonreuters.com/1-382-3382?transitionType=Default&contextData=(sc.Default)

22. https://www.investopedia.com/terms/d/debtfinancing.asp

23. https://www.sapling.com/8084300/debt-redemption

24. https://www.investopedia.com/terms/d/discountrate.asp

25. https://www.divestopedia.com/definition/919/divesting

26. https://www.divestopedia.com/definition/4930/drag-along-rights

27. https://ilpa.org/glossary/drag-along-rights/

28. https://ilpa.org/glossary/tag-along-rights-rights-of-co-sale/

29. https://www.divestopedia.com/definition/6034/dry-powder

30. https://www.pwc.com/us/en/industries/private-equity/library/dual-track-exit-considerations.html

31. https://www.divestopedia.com/definition/724/earnout

32. https://www.economist.com/special-report/2017/10/05/defining-emerging-markets

33. https://www.investopedia.com/terms/e/emergingmarketeconomy.asp

34. https://www.thebalance.com/definition-of-encumbrance-1798545

35. https://www.investopedia.com/terms/e/encumbranc
    e.asp

36. Schumpeter, Joseph A. Essays on Entrepreneurs, Innovations, Business Cycles, and the Evolution of Capitalism. Edited by Richard V. Clemence. 2006.

37. Oslo Manual. Guidelines for Collecting, Reporting and Using Data on Innovation, 4th Edition. OECD. 2018.

38. https://centers.fuqua.duke.edu/cei/eta/

39. https://www.investopedia.com/terms/e/equity.asp

40. https://www.investopedia.com/ask/answers/111414/
    what-difference-between-enterprise-value-and-
    equity-value.asp

41. https://www.investopedia.com/terms/e/escrow.asp

42. https://www.divestopedia.com/definition/844/holdba
    ck

43. http://www.gsi-alliance.org/wp-
    content/uploads/2017/03/GSIR_Review2016.F.pdf

44. https://www.empea.org/research/empea-brief-first-
    time-funds-in-emerging-markets/

45. https://www.investopedia.com/terms/f/funding-
    gap.asp

46. https://www.investopedia.com/terms/g/gdp.asp

47. https://www.mergersandinquisitions.com/definitive-
    agreement-mergers-acquisitions/

48. https://www.investopedia.com/terms/g/goodwill.asp
49. https://www.ictsd.org/what-is-hard-cap-private-equity/
50. https://www.investopedia.com/terms/h/hurdlerate.asp
51. https://www.divestopedia.com/definition/6033/key-man-provision
52. https://www.investopedia.com/terms/l/leveragedbuyout.asp
53. https://www.dcslegal.com/news-and-insights/good-leaverbad-leaver-provisions-%E2%80%93-what-are-they-and-why-do-they-matter
54. https://www.investopedia.com/terms/l/leveragedrecapitalization.asp
55. https://ilpa.org/private-equity-explained/
56. https://lucasktlee.com/2014/08/27/introduction-to-private-equity-fund-terms
57. https://www.investopedia.com/terms/m/mbi.asp
58. https://www.divestopedia.com/2/7839/maximize-value/mezzanine-financing-and-investing-explained
59. https://www.divestopedia.com/definition/4795/micro-private-equity
60. https://docs.preqin.com/reports/Dechert_Preqin_Transaction_and_Monitoring_Fees.pdf

61. https://www.investopedia.com/ask/answers/04/0326
    04.asp
62. https://academic.oup.com/icsidreview/article-
    abstract/30/1/217/719194
63. https://www.italaw.com/sites/default/files/case-
    documents/italaw9921.pdf
64. https://www.newtonequity.com/
65. Heston, S.; Kelly, P. 2020 Search Fund Study: Selected
    Observations. Center for Entrepreneurial Studies at
    the Stanford Graduate School of Business. 2020.
66. https://www.investopedia.com/terms/o/otc.asp
67. https://www.investopedia.com/terms/a/actual-
    owner.asp
68. https://www.cambridge.org/core/books/practical-
    guide-to-private-equity-transactions/publictoprivate-
    transactions/30AC5F384ECBA2FCD6A4D5F320329FBF
69. https://www.investopedia.com/terms/p/payoutratio.
    asp
70. https://www.divestopedia.com/definition/4965/ratch
    et
71. https://www.investopedia.com/articles/stocks/09/intr
    oduction-reverse-mergers.asp
72. https://www.divestopedia.com/definition/1119/rolled
    -equity

73. https://www.valuationresearch.com/pure-perspectives/rollover-equity-private-equity-deals/
74. https://www.investopedia.com/terms/r/restricted-stock-unit.asp
75. https://www.callan.com/blog-archive/pe-measurement/
76. https://www.mccannfitzgerald.com/knowledge/start-ups/simple-agreements-for-future-equity-what-are-they-and-how-can-they-be-used
77. https://www.gsb.stanford.edu/experience/about/centers-institutes/ces/research/search-funds
78. https://www.investopedia.com/terms/s/secondary-buyout.asp
79. https://www.divestopedia.com/definition/787/vendor-financing
80. https://www.divestopedia.com/definition/5061/shareholders-agreement
81. https://www.investopedia.com/terms/s/smallandmidsizeenterprises.asp
82. https://www.investopedia.com/terms/s/spac.asp
83. https://www.investopedia.com/terms/s/succession.asp
84. https://www.divestopedia.com/definition/5132/sweet-equity

85. https://www.divestopedia.com/definition/4950/term-sheet

86. https://www.morganlewis.com/pubs/2016/03/considerations-in-transition-services-agreements-in-ma-transactions

87. https://www.investopedia.com/terms/t/turnaround.asp

88. https://www.investopedia.com/terms/u/unlistedsecurity.asp

89. https://www.investopedia.com/terms/v/vesting.asp

90. https://www.investopedia.com/terms/w/wacc.asp

91. https://en.wikipedia.org/wiki/Distribution_waterfall

92. https://www.investopedia.com/terms/p/pledgefund.asp

93. https://www.investopedia.com/terms/a/agencycosts.asp#

94. https://www.investopedia.com/terms/m/mba.asp

\*\*\*

Printed in Great Britain
by Amazon